#Unsubscribed

A teenager choosing to live without social media in this age of technology? Seems impossible. And yet, here I am.

Beginning in fifth grade, I have been battling with myself about whether or not I wanted to use social media. Join me as I lay out my journey of deciding to be **unsubscribed.**

Our society is complicated. We have problems and we don't always think to give ourselves the space to answer the questions life throws at us. Instead, we use every spare moment to update our stories, check our feeds, and respond to our latest snaps. Join me as I reveal the thoughts of our generation that are often left **unspoken.**

We can be consumed by our virtual profiles and we don't always know the best way to step back. Join me as I articulate practical strategies for discovering how to use social media in moderation.

We may feel like victims to our devices, but we don't have to be. We can choose to be **unstoppable.**

#Unsubscribed

*How I am thriving in high
school without social media
(and you can, too)*

Alexa Mendes

First paperback edition July 2019
Cover photo by Val Vesa
Cover design by Alexa & Susan Mendes

ISBN 978-1-0806-0952-9 (paperback)
www.unsubscribedbook.weebly.com
unsubscribedbook@gmail.com

PRAISE FOR
ALEXA MENDES'
#UNSUBSCRIBED

"Using personal narrative infused with insight, Alexa Mendes provides a deeper dive into the Gen Z experience of social media. While the scientific field is scrambling to understand how social media impacts youth mental health and social development, and mainstream media interest is intense – detailed discussion and practical guidance for young people and parents are often lacking. #Unsubscribed provides a window into what might surprise many – that teens are thoughtfully grappling with how their use of social media impacts them, their thought life and sense of self, and the strategies they are finding to best achieve balance."

**- Christine Moutier, M.D.
Chief Medical Officer,
American Foundation for
Suicide Prevention**

"This book is a game changer if you wish to regain the appreciation of the natural world. A must read, especially for the amazing teenagers and young adults that live in despair because of social media."

**- Dr. Francisco Escobedo, Award-Winning
Elementary School District Superintendent**

TABLE OF CONTENTS

CONTENTS

INTRODUCTION

#Unsubscribed

INTRODUCTION

One score and nine years ago, the founding fathers of this modern era invented the internet, with social media platforms following shortly thereafter. My life, and yours, have been shaped by a result of these creations. It is time to address the truth: we are addicted to social media. This book is an invitation to become aware of the effects it has on our lives and move forward, consciously choosing how we utilize it.

By writing this book, I also want to bring light to the fact that social media is not essential for thriving in this modern world. Although this statement may seem ridiculous, it is the truth. And I am living proof. I am a part of the first generation who has *grown up* with social media--I can hardly remember a time without it-- and yet, I choose not to actively use social media.

Even though I have made this choice, I am not isolated from social activity. On the contrary, I am extremely involved in my community. For example, I made our high school's Varsity girls basketball team as both a freshman and a sophomore. Our team won the regional championship in freshman year for the first time in our school's history. I was named Student of the Year at both my elementary and middle schools. I have played on many club basketball teams and have won multiple championships. I have actively participated in student government since fifth grade. I gave a school-wide speech and was elected as our high school's Sophomore Director, and therefore planned our school's winter formal (approximately 1000 students attended!). I volunteer at my church. I have earned my Girl Scout Bronze, Silver, and Gold Awards (the highest award a Girl Scout can earn).

Furthermore, this summer (as a rising high school junior), I was accepted to attend the 8-week summer quarter at Stanford University (through the Stanford High School Summer Session program). However, I tore my ACL playing club basketball a few weeks before I was to leave, so I was unable to participate in my dream summer of taking neuroscience and writing classes, staying in the dorms, and living the college life. Instead, I am focused on doing physical therapy and having surgery on my knee. Realizing I had more free time than I was expecting, I took the opportunity to write this book.

The reason I am sharing these achievements with you is not to brag or boast; I hope to show with what I have accomplished that social media is not essential to success. I am a teenager in the midst of a society in which social media is an integral aspect of daily life, and yet I choose not to use it. With my experiences both using and not using these networking sites, I can provide authentic, valuable, and unusual insights and perspectives regarding a topic that overshadows our civilization.

However, I am fully aware that I am not the only one with such experiences concerning social media. In fact, while in the process of writing this book, I asked some of my peers how they felt about social media. Their feedback has inspired me in my writing, as many of us shared similar perspectives. At the beginning of each chapter, I have included some of their responses to this simple, yet complicated question: "How do you feel about social media?". Their responses add depth and context, helping you further connect with the experiences and ideas in this book.

Every era has its own set of dilemmas. In our time, we are facing the evident effects of social media: stress, anxiety, and suicide rates are on the rise. I am here to be the voice to express what is often left unspoken. I wrote this book with the hope that it would provide encouragement, tips, and validation to all who, like me, are doing their best to live a balanced life in this generation of social media.

PART ONE
Unsubscribed

*To use, or not to use. That is the question.
Throughout my elementary, middle, and
high school years, I have chosen to both use
and not use social media. In this first
section, I describe my journey ultimately
deciding not to have an active presence on
social media and how I am thriving
without it.*

#Unsubscribed

1: PLAYING THE COMPARISON GAME

"Social media is honestly a double edged sword for me - that's why I don't use it often. I think it starts to get to people when you see yourself unnecessarily comparing your life to others all the time through only happy posts."
-Taylor, age 16

#Unsubscribed

1

Growing up, using social media was a choice. My parents never told me I couldn't use it, and allowed me to forge my own understanding of it. I am so grateful to have had this freedom and opportunity to learn about social media from my own choices and experiences.

Beginning in fifth grade, I was extremely active on social media (mainly Instagram and Snapchat). As not many of my friends had access to these networks, I spent the majority of my time fangirling over One Direction and planning my imagined future with Louis Tomlinson.

Right around the time when I was completely immersed in my obsession with using social media and following One Direction, the season of Lent was coming. As a Catholic Christian, we observe the season of Lent (the 40 days leading up to Easter) as a solemn time of reflection as we remember the 40 days Jesus spent in the desert. It is a common practice to give up something we enjoy (in order that we may be joined closer to Christ in His sufferings, both in the desert and on the cross) and/or add a new habit of spiritual growth in its place. As something that took up the majority of my every spare moment, I decided to give up using Instagram and Snapchat for Lent.

The first couple of days after I deleted the apps, I was overwhelmed and basically going through withdrawals. Every couple of seconds, I would pick up my phone and swipe to the place where Instagram and Snapchat used to be, realize they were not there, and blindly stare at the screen for a few moments. A few minutes later, I would do the same thing, expecting the apps to have magically reappeared on my phone. It was just like looking at the refrigerator when we're hungry: first we look in the fridge to see what's in there. If nothing looks good, maybe we'll go check the cupboards. Nothing in the cupboards? Better check the fridge again. Unsurprisingly, nothing had changed, the same foods were still in the fridge that were there two minutes ago. Likewise, no matter how many times I checked, the same apps were still missing from my device.

Throughout these 40 days of Lent, I slowly grew accustomed to life without social media. The usual constant checking of Snapchat to ensure that my streaks were alive and well, always wanting to make sure my Snapchat story was fun and interesting, the constant Instagram stream of thought *(What picture should I post next on Instagram? Which filter should I use? Nobody likes overly filtered photos, but at the same time there are some nice ones on VSCO that people seem to be using... What caption should I use? Make sure it's not too cliche, but it should fit in with what's socially relevant. Which hashtags do I include? How would this post fit in with the overall look of my feed? Should I add a hint of color when I edit it to make it more aesthetic? When was the last time I posted? Am I posting too often? Or not often enough? I don't want to turn into a ghost follower...then people might not let me follow them! Are my number of followers and people I'm following balanced? Should I let that person follow me? Should I follow that person back?)*, and the anticipation of receiving likes and comments in response to my postings slowly began to fade. I was no longer sitting in the Instagram app, refreshing my feed every five seconds hoping someone had posted something new. I was no longer watching all of the Snapchat stories of my friends, ESPN, BuzzFeed and all of the other companies that provided daily entertainment. Social media no longer controlled my life.

At the end of the 40-day period, I was hesitant to re-install Instagram and Snapchat on my phone. However, I eventually decided to use it again, but told myself I would try to limit my use. It was overwhelming trying to catch back up with all of the missed posts--my feed was so long! There had even been updates to both apps, which I now had to figure out how to use and incorporate into my posts (talk about stressful!).

Time continued, and so did my presence on these networks. As a middle schooler, it was demanding trying to figure out life at a new school, a new system of classes, making new friends, and trying to figure out who I was. Not to mention, like most middle schoolers, I needed to figure out how to best represent myself on Instagram and Snapchat to make myself appear "cool," all while trying to stay true to myself (and, like most, I didn't really know who I was at that point).

I began to realize that, not only was I spending too much time on these apps, but every time I went on them I felt worse afterwards. I eventually understood: I was playing the comparison game. Instagram, for me, was all about trying to impress others. It was almost like I thought, if I could trick them into thinking that I was "cool," maybe I would think that I was "cool," too. The problem was, I never felt like I looked good enough in my photos, they weren't artsy enough, and I never quite reached that "cool" standard. Then I would look at everyone else's feeds and they would seem like models in a photoshoot.

Every time I went on Instagram, and even Snapchat (looking at people's stories), I was playing this comparison game. The other problem was, this game was completely rigged. I was always comparing my entire life (problems, insecurities, weaknesses) with everyone else's highlight reel. I am also an extremely competitive person (by the way, did I mention my Varsity basketball team won the regional championship freshman year?), so I felt unsatisfied unless I could find some way to "win" at something. But with the comparison game, I never won.

My dad always told me, "Comparison is the fast track to misery." Never had I felt the truth of this statement more than when I used social media. Why did I continue using it? For one main reason: I didn't want to feel left out. Looking back, I would say that I definitely had FOMO: the fear of missing out.

It was a rather paradoxical situation: I didn't want to stop using social media because I didn't want to feel excluded. Yet the exclusion I felt as a result of using social media was one of the reasons I didn't like it. Looking at my friends' Snapchat stories was particularly troublesome. I wanted to be in-the-know in case something important was happening with them. Plus, I always wanted to clear the notifications of having unwatched stories. But at the same time, I also felt a gut-wrenching betrayal when I saw a group of my closest friends hanging out and I wasn't invited. This almost always left me in an awkward situation: I wanted to let them know I felt left out (I would debate sending the classic, passive aggressive *no invite?* text), but at the same time, I could understand if they wanted to hang out in a smaller group. However, that did not ease the pain of feeling excluded, so I usually left Snapchat feeling empty.

The exclusion I'm referring to is also a two-way street. If I was hanging out with some friends, I would feel rather uncomfortable when I noticed them putting pictures and videos on their story. I would also try to ignore my own guilt while updating my feed or uploading the latest funny moment to my story, because I knew that other people who were watching my story were probably also feeling the sense of betrayal I had mentioned earlier.

The comparison game is much like the movie *Nerve*. In this movie, the protagonist begins playing a game that seems to be merely a fun competition. Before long, she finds that she is trapped in the game and it is controlling her every move; in other words, the game took over her life. With social media, I began using it just for fun, simply as a way to follow One Direction accounts. As such networks increased in popularity, I began thinking about the sites more and more. The comparison game was then ingrained into my life in a way that, even when I was not using the apps, I was still thinking about them; I was always on the lookout for the next thing I could post to my story.

I was a victim of the comparison game.

2: THE SELF-CONTROL MUSCLE

"Social media has its goods and bads, but most of it is negative. I'm not using social media at the moment, but I think that it's such a big part of society and our generation that it's difficult not being on it."
-Alyssa, age 16

#Unsubscribed

2

Thankfully, self-control was one of the skills I had developed throughout my childhood. Every year for Lent, I would challenge myself to give up something I truly loved. Although it is not supposed to be a time to prove how strong your self-control is, as a naive child unaware of the spiritual reasons for fasting, these 40-days became a way for me to practice improving my self-control. For example, when I was much younger, I gave up watching TV for Lent. This may not seem like much, but for a child who was only six-years-old, it was a feat. Before Lent, my routine was to treat myself to watching TV on Saturday morning every weekend. By choosing to give up TV for the 40-day period, I was pushing myself to grow my ability to use self-control.

In the following years, I also gave up treats. I remember one time in particular, I went with a few friends to watch my one friend's theatre performance. Afterwards, her mom took the group of us out to celebrate with frozen yogurt. It would have been so easy to give in (the toppings looked delicious!), but I knew that this was an opportunity to further deepen my self-control. I made my decision and I stuck to it: I did not have frozen yogurt that night, even though it meant setting myself apart from the group. I was willing to remove myself from that group's norm of having frozen yogurt, because I knew that was the best decision for me.

Self-control is like a muscle. The more you use it, the stronger it becomes. With all the practice I had successfully completed throughout my years of fasting during Lent, I knew I was ready for game day. The competitors? The comparison game against me. The only prize? My time, thoughts, and self esteem. In essence, we were playing for control over my life.

In eighth grade, I made the first move -- the apps were deleted. With the coming days and weeks, the comparison game fought back with the same symptoms of withdrawal I felt during my practice round in Lent: repeatedly checking my phone (like a refrigerator), trying to check my apps before realizing they weren't there, time spent staring at a blank screen, and the doubts that I was making a mistake and I was going to become an antisocial outcast without them. I definitely thought about reinstalling these apps, but my self-control muscle reminded me of all the other times I had previously maintained my endurance in similar situations. The apps remained deleted.

As time passed, the concept of living without social media slowly normalized. I experienced less and less urges to use social media as I began to fill the hole with other tasks like playing solitaire with real cards, learning a new song on the piano, playing the ukulele, training my dogs, reading, and learning how to solve a Rubik's cube.

Although the transition was not perfect (I did feel left out sometimes--but again, it is one of those paradoxical situations), I ultimately finished what I started. In a world where social media is central to most people's lives, I proved it doesn't have to be. For thousands of years, people survived without technology. Although it is now ingrained into our schools and workplaces, it is definitely possible to live without social media.

3: FREEDOM IN TRULY LIVING

"I want to delete it, but I can't because it's how I advertise my business, how I socialize, and how I get information...When I went to [camp] and disconnected it was awesome, but when we got reception it was stressful."
-Wesley, age 16

#Unsubscribed

3

The lack of activity on social media has given me the freedom to explore life and relationships for what they really are. Drowning in thoughts about my next post, how my story looks, and who's follow request I should accept was consuming. Now, however, there is so much more time and brain space that I can explore.

One of the refreshing aspects of not actively using social media is that it helps foster more intimate friendships. For example, if someone posts an invitation to their birthday party on their Snapchat story, you can never really know if they want you to be there. If you don't use social media, the person has to personally invite you; if they make that extra effort, there is no doubt that you are wanted at that party.

It is also interesting to walk up to a group of people and notice that they are all on their phones, and aren't really talking to each other. How weird! Instead of spending time with the people by our sides, we prefer to be on our phones, talking to other people online. It's almost a nonverbal way of saying, "I'd rather be spending time with these people online than with you in person." Without social media, I am not nearly as tempted to be on my phone when I am with other people, allowing me to dive into deeper conversations and create more meaningful relationships.

Not using social media has also helped me to enjoy the moment. Before, when I used social media, if I were doing something noteworthy (or just something ordinary), I would press pause on the actual moment in order to ensure that I captured it perfectly to post on my story. Now (although I may briefly capture the moment in an imperfect photo, since I know I won't be posting it), I can focus more on the moment itself. Instead of trying to utilize the beauty or the humor around me, I can simply soak it in. I no longer have to feed my feed, I only need to feed my own needs. I am free to truly live.

***

Every summer, my family and I have a tradition of spending a week in the mountains at a family camp. The natural scenery is unbelievable. During the day, the trees stretch so high it makes our necks crack to look all the way up to the top. We can hear the gushing creek flowing from our cabin, and see the height and depth of the surrounding mountains. We can see the crisp blue sky and feel the warmth of the sun radiating off our skin. We feel like we're on top of the world as we climb to the top of the challenge course, zipline, giant swing, or after a hike. The smooth, turquoise waters of the lake provide a reprieve from the hot sand. We can experience flight as we bounce off one end of a giant, floating pillow (also known as a blob) as a friend provides the counteracting weight at the other end. We can taste the most delicious milkshakes ever made. We can feel that underlying sense of excitement and fear as the suspension bridge swings while we walk across it. We can hear the chatter and clanking of silverware in the dining hall. At night, we can hear the crickets chirping in the silence. We can see more stars in the sky than we imagined possible. The sense of community is overwhelming. The joy in the air is tangible.

Some of my favorite memories come from both participating and volunteering at this family camp. It truly is a retreat, and everyone leaves feeling refreshed from a memorable week. Each year, there is one item absent from my packing list: my social media. When I had social media, I didn't bring my device to camp. Now, while I no longer use social media, I use my phone mainly as a clock and a camera. The absence of constant technology in this camp is one of the underlying reasons why it is so incredible: without the distraction of social media, we are free to create lasting friendships and memories. We are not tied down by the urge to update our stories, keep up our streaks, or like our friends' latest posts. All of those things can wait. At camp, we are focused on enjoying life moment by moment.

I couldn't wait to give back to the place that had given so much to me. After seventh grade (when I still actively used social media), I volunteered as a child care assistant (CCA). As CCAs, we were required to give up our phones to our head counselor upon arrival, as a way to get the most out of the camp experience.

After yet another phenomenal week of rejuvenation, my cabin mates and I were packing our belongings to head down the mountain. Our counselor brought out the case with our phones and told us we were free to retrieve them. I will never forget the chatter amongst the girls as we were asked to take our phones: we were all talking about how we didn't want them back. A group of teenage girls, who were hesitant to relinquish their phones at the beginning of the week, did not want them back.

Without our phones, we were free from distractions. We cultivated meaningful friendships (that were by no means based on status or number of followers). We weren't so caught up with impressing our followers that we were able to enjoy nature, each others' presence, real conversations, and authentic friendships. By letting go of social media for merely one week, we were truly living.

4: THE VACUUM

*"It kind of takes control of people's lives
sometimes. It can be a great thing if used
sparingly, but that never really happens
because it's so addicting. It's so sad to me how
much time people waste on it."*
- Paxton, age 16

#Unsubscribed

4

The absence of social media has given me so much more time, greatly increasing my productivity. As most teenagers are, I can be a master procrastinator. Also like most teenagers, I know I shouldn't procrastinate, but then I do it anyway. Besides, how much harm could come from checking your phone one last time before writing that essay? While I still was still active on Snapchat and Instagram, these apps became another way for me to procrastinate. If I didn't want to do something, I would check my Instagram. When I finished looking through new posts on my feed (and refreshing it a couple of times, just to be sure), I transitioned into the explore section. The title for the explore section does not do it justice--although it may start out with simply exploring, it eventually turns into a vacuum.

By clicking on the explore tab you might see a paint mixing video. It looks satisfying, so you click on it to see the aesthetic in full screen. Then you start to wonder what other types of videos that account has, and proceed to scroll through their feed. At some point, you notice an interesting comment with the username of some Harry Potter fanfiction account. Intrigued, you click on their page and begin scrolling through their fan art, conspiracy theories, and countless fanfiction stories. Eventually, as you find yourself looking at photos from three years ago on a nature photography account, you look up at the clock. An hour has passed and you still haven't started that essay. What happened? You were sucked into the depths of the vacuum.

Or perhaps you are more of a Snapchat person. Sometimes I was, too. You would find yourself opening one quick snap from a friend before studying for your math exam. Just one snap can't hurt, right? Then you would find yourself immersed in a serious (or seriously funny) snap conversation that lasted for a half an hour. Then you would realize there had been a new update and you needed to check out all of the new filters! Suddenly your heart skips a beat: there's a timer emoji next to your longest streak with your best friend! Quick, better send them streaks. While you're at it, you might as well send streaks to all of your friends (possibly complaining about all the math studying you still haven't started yet). One of them responds, and you can't just leave them on read (obviously, they're your number one best friend!), so another conversation develops. An hour has passed and you still haven't started studying. What happened? You were sucked into the depths of the vacuum.

It is also possible that you have already started your homework, determined to finish it at a reasonable hour this time. There you are, working away; one problem done, halfway through the next--must be time for a brain break! You pick up your phone and prepare to attend to all of your notifications, but you realize you don't have any because you already responded to them five minutes ago. You still feel the need for a brain break, though, and you proceed to the discover section of Snapchat. There is so much to catch up on! From the obnoxious number detailing the stories you have yet to see (that can only be cleared by watching them), to the different magazine-like daily feeds from Cosmopolitan and ESPN you have yet to explore! Finally, you finish looking through all your friends' stories and are left feeling excluded (why are they all hanging out without you?). Now you're *really* not in the mood to finish the rest of your homework. That's when the magazine-like daily feeds come into play! After learning the latest life hacks from Cosmopolitan, celebrity gossip from People Magazine, and taken too many BuzzFeed quizzes to count (who knew what you eat for breakfast can tell you when you're getting married?), you're emotionally exhausted. Plus, your evening has gone by in a flash, you still have homework to do, and you feel empty. What happened? You were sucked into the depths of the vacuum.

Having been sucked into the vacuum on numerous occasions (and having plenty of experiences with all of the examples above), I can attest to the detrimental effects social media can have on productivity. It is so easy to allow yourself to enter the vacuum, but it takes a lot of willpower (or the headache and other symptoms that come with so much scrolling) to leave it.

***

One day, I was in my carpool on the way to school and the dad who was driving us asked us what we would choose if we could have anything in the world. I responded with time, as I was feeling overwhelmed with all that I needed to do with my projects, sports, and schoolwork. He then responded that it is not that we need more time, it's that we need to be more cognizant of how we use the time that we do have. My experience with the time I have gained by not using social media has taught me exactly that.

I am no longer tempted by these vacuums and the amount of time I used to spend on social media is now free for me to use for my liking. For example, while I was completing my Girl Scout Gold Award, I was also in the middle of our Varsity basketball season, all while simultaneously planning our school's winter formal (we had around 1,000 kids attend!). Needless to say, it was a pretty hectic season that required a lot of time management. Because I didn't have the procrastination tool of social media, I was able to focus on each of these activities individually, while still maintaining my normal sleep schedule, keeping up with all of my schoolwork, and staying healthy. It's hard to believe how much time I spent on social media, until I had it all back.

5: SETBACKS

"I think we just need to get better at using it. Mankind has never been able to stay in contact so far and fast nor have we [been] able to spread awareness so much...but that's why we have texting...there's so much more to life than just bragging about your fake life and hiding the truth and your insecurities."
-Anabelle, age 15

#Unsubscribed

5

Not using social media has been one of the best decisions I have ever made. However, that doesn't mean that there haven't been aspects of this decision that weren't ideal either. For example, many people use Instagram and Snapchat to keep in touch with long distance family members, form group chats, stay in the loop with current events happening at school or workplaces, and share funny pictures and videos. Even though I can't replicate these exact experiences, I am able to do them in my own way.

For example, one of my cousins lives in another state and I used to keep in touch with her by using Snapchat. Now, we make the extra effort to check in with each other through texting. Even though we may not communicate as much, the interactions that we do have are much more genuine. In other words, instead of sending each other random pictures for streaks everyday, we have more meaningful conversations about what is actually going on in our lives.

Likewise, I have friends who live in other countries, and we are limited in our communication due to my lack of social media activity. However, this only improves our friendship because when we text each other, we know we are purposely thinking about the other. The texts are more thoughtful and, again, help us to share exactly what's going on in our lives instead of sending random pictures to keep a streak going.

In my opinion, one of the biggest hindrances of not being active on social media is the use of Instagram and Snapchat group chats. However, if you are accessing social media on a phone, there is always the option of group chats over text. Additionally, if there is a hilarious post that friends are looking at, they can always share it with you through screenshotting, screen recording, and sending links.

Finally, the other main challenge I have faced by not using social media is the lack of awareness of events that are going on at school or in the workplace. Nonetheless, like all of the other setbacks that come with a lack of participation on social media, there is a solution: setting limits.

#Unsubscribed

6: LIMITS

"Social media can obviously be a good thing and a bad thing... a lot of people don't know when it stops being a good thing for them...I took a break from all my social medias for awhile because I had gotten into a few bad habits that weren't good for me and weren't making me happy...the limited use is good for me now in my life...a lot of people use social media blindly without thinking about the impact it's having on them, or don't care enough to actually think about it."
-Grace, age 19

#Unsubscribed

6

As an ASB (Associated Student Body/ student government) enthusiast who has planned many events, including our school's winter formal, I love to know what's going on at my school. Being involved with and participating in as many events as possible to grow closer to my school and community is a part of who I am. When I was in the ASB class, it was easy to stay connected and aware of upcoming events, as we were the ones planning them. However, when I was not in ASB, I realized that Instagram was one of the main ways ASB connected with and informed the student body of ways they could be involved. As most of the students use Instagram, the majority of people were aware of the various events being publicized through this media outlet. Although other methods were also used for these announcements, Instagram was the main stream of communication.

On various occasions, I would notice that people were talking about school events that had happened recently of which I was unaware. Once again, I was facing feelings of exclusion--especially because being involved at school is such a fundamental aspect of my personality.

Still not wanting to be active on social media, I tried to problem solve. I didn't like what was happening, but I also didn't want to change my actions. Realizing I would need to compromise, I decided I would use Instagram under the following three conditions:

1. I would keep the Instagram app off my phone.

2. I would only look at accounts that would give me informative updates, such as our school's student life account, our basketball team account, or a specific friend or family member's account if I knew they were traveling. After viewing the specific accounts I had planned to look at, I would log off.

3. I would not like, comment, or post anything while I was looking at the few specific accounts.

By using these three techniques, I was setting myself up for success. The limitations allowed me to both obtain the relevant information I felt like I was previously missing out on, while still avoiding falling into my old habits.

The first guideline forces me to think twice before logging on because I have to do the extra step of going through the internet. Thus, if I was going to spend time on Instagram, I had to do it consciously. With the second ground rule, I was preventing myself from getting sucked into the vacuum of the explore section and from getting caught up in playing the comparison game. Lastly, the third custom relieved me of the mental wear and tear social media had previously brought me. I was eliminating the pain of having constant streams of thought (how aesthetic my feed looked, which posts I should like, what to comment on those posts, who to follow, who to let follow me, etc.) by removing myself from activity. Not to mention, it would be rather odd if I only logged on once in a while and then went on a liking, commenting, and posting spree -- people would be confused as to whether or not they should tag me and ask to follow me. Plus, since I only would be logging in once in awhile, it is fairly likely that I would be looking at people's posts from a few days (or even weeks or months) back, and it is seen as stalking to be active on such posts. Liking, commenting, and posting would just make things difficult, misleading, and awkward.

These self-made regulations have been the perfect compromise: I am able to stay in the loop and be informed with our latest school and team events while still removing myself from the addictive and negative habits I had formerly developed. (Plus, as a bonus feature, I am able to continue strengthening my self-control muscle by holding myself accountable to these norms.) I continue to use these regulations today, as they have become my perfect moderation.

#Unsubscribed

PART TWO
Unspoken

Social media plays a huge role in the functioning of our society today. However, we don't always take the time to think about how it may be affecting us personally. In part two, I share my thoughts about various aspects of social media. You may or may not agree with my ideas, but either way is fantastic and I thank you for being open to another perspective. Often times we only hear the perspectives of the powerful celebrities and companies, so the purpose of this section is to reveal my point of view on social media; I hope to provide a voice for those who don't feel heard. I want to bring light to the thoughts of many which are often left unspoken.

#Unsubscribed

7: SILENCE

"It can be good to connect with people, but it lowers many people's self esteem and most of it is just people trying to act like someone they aren't, especially Instagram. I should really take a break from it because it is kind of pointless."
-Grant, age 16

#Unsubscribed

7

Loneliness is an epidemic in our society. The overall mental health of our population has been decreasing over the past few decades. The suicide rates continue to rise. Hearing these types of statements in various discussions and on the news is extremely upsetting. Many of us are concerned about the future of our society.

There is so much going on in the world today; it would be unfair to peg all of the problems on a single cause. However, it is also important to begin addressing these issues in order to be able to make changes. I wonder if the addiction many of us have to social media is playing a role in this downfall.

As a Girl Scout, I earned the Gold Award by adhering to the structured format Girl Scouts has provided to help ensure our success. The project process is broken down into seven steps: choose an issue, investigate, get help, create a plan, present your plan, take action, and educate & inspire. The goal is to find an issue you are passionate about and then find a way to make a lasting impact within that issue. After 11 years of Girl Scouting, I couldn't wait to get started with my project. The trouble was, I had no idea what issue I wanted to choose and how I could make a sustainable change.

After changing my mind multiple times (in a similar manner as undergraduate students picking their major), I resolved to tackle the issue of stress. After picking this topic, the next step was to identify the root causes (so that we would be able to create sustainable change). For my project, I established that the lack of awareness of healthy stress management was a root cause of stress. From there I was able to create and execute my project, ultimately earning the Girl Scout equivalent of an Eagle Scout Award.

Now, what's the connection between the concerns of increased loneliness, the rising number of suicides, declining mental health, and the process of achieving the Girl Scout Gold Award? They all deal with global problems. And the best way to combat such problems is by exploring resolutions that address their root causes.

What is the root cause of all of these problems? That is the million-dollar question. Although there are undoubtedly many variables to take into consideration while evaluating this extensive question, I have noticed one uniting factor: we are afraid of silence.

***

Everyday is busier than the last. As a high schooler, I am in the midst of what seems to be millions of expectations. Colleges no longer expect 4.0 grade point averages, they are looking for 5.0 GPAs. Not to mention, they also want students who are committed to various extracurricular activities, play Varsity sports, have jobs, pursue internships, and participate in honors societies. And remember, we are only in high school for four years! So we definitely need to include time for enjoyment and fun, too (hanging out with friends, going to school games together, going to the dances, and so much more). In the midst of this busy time, we don't want to waste a second.

The problem is, when we keep running on the hamster wheel, trying to accomplish as much as possible (and get a semi-reasonable amount of sleep) while still enjoying ourselves, we grow accustomed to continual busyness. Moreover, when we do have a spare second to collect our thoughts, we reach for our phones out of habit. Whether it is browsing social media, checking for email updates, watching a quick YouTube video, or texting a friend, we have an inherent urge to remain occupied. Why? We are afraid of silence.

When was the last time you did nothing? No technology, no homework, no projects, no work, no talking; only being present in the moment. Being able to sit alone with ourselves is *incredibly* difficult, and is often uncomfortable. When we sit with our own thoughts, and face reality, we feel like we need to be accomplishing something (even if that something is procrastinating).

All day, we are being bombarded by the ideas, beliefs, and opinions of friends, teachers, co-workers, and newscasters. We spend time with so many people. Especially in an age of social media, we are exposed to so much. Often times, this exposure can be positive! It can help raise awareness of a non-profit organization, help connect friends and family who live far away, and be a great place to share ideas. But after looking at so many other people's thoughts, do we truly know our own beliefs?

If you **take one thing away from this book**, I hope it is to **spend time in silence** (even though it's challenging). Without any distractions, we can really get to know who we are as a unique person, and better understand our own feelings (even when it may feel scary and awkward). Spending time in silence also gives us the opportunity to reflect on our day and find reasons to be grateful (which improves mental health).

The other thing about silence is that nobody can do it for us; it is something that we have to do for ourselves. Once, when I was younger and I was sick and feeling awful, my mom told me that if she could, she would take the sickness from me and bear it instead. As that was not an option, there was no way around it: I needed to face it myself. Likewise, even though spending time in distraction-free silence isn't always the most appealing option, no one else can face silence for us. We are ultimately the only ones who can do it. And the choice as to whether or not we do is a choice only we can make.

We make time for things we find important to us. Do you value your mental health? Do you find worth in knowing who you are as a person? Do you think it is meaningful to know your personal beliefs?

Silence is calling. Will you answer?

8: LONELINESS

*"I feel it's a great way of communication and
to see what your friends are doing and stay
connected, but also can be very hurtful to your
self image and make you feel self conscious
and worse about your life and
the person you are."
-Hudson, age 15*

#Unsubscribed

8

Our generation seems to be facing a loneliness crisis, and one of my theories is that we have lost the art of building genuine relationships. Social media provides us with a platform to communicate with friends and family across the world (I have friends and family who live in different states and countries, so I'm in the same boat). Unfortunately, we also use it so much that we lose opportunities to connect with the people who are right next to us.

As a society, we spend more time getting to know the edited and perfected versions of people as they portray themselves online, instead of really getting to know who they are with their strengths *and* weaknesses, their joys *and* sorrows. We have many followers, but we may never have interacted with them in real life. Yes, we may be able to connect more, but we aren't doing enough connecting; social media seems to be multiplying our loneliness.

Especially in the teenage years, we are fighting to face insecurities, trying to figure out who we are, and learning how to live as we approach adulthood. Everyone feels lonely at some point or another; many of us (myself included) have looked to social media during these times when we felt isolated to try to fill our feelings of emptiness by interacting with others. Yet, in my experience, I always felt *more* lonely after using social media to try and *rid* myself of loneliness. Why? Those interactions were merely superficial.

Social media sites also provide a platform on which people can cyberbully, causing horrible emotional pain. It is easier for bullies to make malicious remarks to a screen, than it is to tell someone the same comment while looking them in the eyes. The option of creating an anonymous account remains, as well. Thus, when people are feeling insecure, they can more easily inflict misery upon others, without the victim being able to find out who said such a thing. Countless children and young adults are bullied at school. I can only imagine what it would be like to come home from a horrible day at school only to find that there is no reprieve: the bullying can continue into the safety of their own home.

Even if the bullying is not a direct crude statement, people can still be deeply wounded by their interactions with others from behind the safety of their screens. For those of you who are unaware, it is very common to do things such as tbh (to be honest, where someone offers to tell you what they actually think of you), rates (usually on a scale of 1-10 or as grades like A, B, C, D, F), hot or not, date or hate, hug or ugh, and first impressions. Especially when people are bored (or are subconsciously trying to do something to avoid facing their innermost realities in silence), this is one of the most common things people do on both Instagram and Snapchat. People would post a picture on their stories saying offering tbhs and rates, and then their followers would respond by DMing (direct messaging) them asking for either, or both.

As a follower, being given such an offer is very tempting. As I mentioned before, we are teenagers in the midst of adolescence. To be able to know exactly what people think of us and not having to wonder is the best case scenario, right? Well, to put it simply, no. After receiving a number of tbhs and rates, I have realized how harmful and awkward these situations are. First of all, the person giving the judgments has to decide whether or not they are going to actually be honest and risk hurting the other person, or lie to them and also risk hurting them.

No matter what the outcome is, the person receiving the tbhs and rates probably would not feel satisfied with their response. If they rated high or gave a nice tbh, the receiver may think it wasn't honest and feel bad. If the rate was low or the tbh was mean, the receiver wouldn't feel good either.

Thus, they feel like they were not good enough and their self-esteem deflates. Unfortunately, when receiving these comments, it feels like the whole world is weighing in. But that is simply not the case: it is only one person's perspective. Hence, the receivers (and really, those giving the judgments, too) are left with the same hole of emptiness and loneliness that they started with, except now it has grown deeper. And our relationship with the person who gave us the judgment probably changed, too.

Not to mention, we still have no idea what the answers to life's big questions are-- in fact, I can fairly say that we are more confused now than before turning to social media--and we don't have close friends who we trust to discuss these questions.

(The content in this chapter was directed at all types of relationships--familial, friendships, romantic relationships, you name it. However, for more information regarding navigation of romantic relationships specifically, I *highly* suggest reading Sarah Swafford's book, *Emotional Virtue*. It changed my life.)

#Unsubscribed

9: WHAT DOES THAT MEAN?

*"I feel like social media is a good tool. I have an
Instagram, but I don't really use it for
'socializing,' mostly looking at art and stuff."
-Nicole, age 15*

#Unsubscribed

9

Being able to communicate effectively is extremely necessary, yet also extremely challenging. Clear communication is essential for all relationships (whether that be student-teacher, doctor-patient, boyfriend-girlfriend, boss-employee, parent-child, friend-friend, or any other combination of people). We need to be able to express ourselves in such a way that the other people can perceive the message we are trying to relay. Unfortunately, when interacting with others, there is always room for miscommunication, which can lead to misunderstandings, and ultimately result in damaged relationships.

In face-to-face interactions, even though it is often challenging to express oneself in a way that is understandable, at least there are certain cues we can look to for help understanding the message others are trying to get across. Body language, facial expressions, and voice intonation can all help us differentiate between a sarcastic comment, and genuine enthusiasm. While interacting online, on the other hand, these identifying factors are not readily accessible and the true intention is often left to the interpretation of the person receiving the information.

For instance, if I were to comment on a friend's Instagram post, "How cool," there are multiple possible interpretations. This simple two-word phrase could be perceived as a passive aggressive comment with the connotation of jealousy, portraying the idea of accusation for not having been invited to whatever event was being captured by that post. On the other hand, it could also be a genuine exclamation acknowledging that the friend's experience appeared to be fantastic! There is no clear way to tell--even with the use of emojis (which could even further the confusion of the intention).

As another example, my friend and I were texting after school one day and she was telling me the story about how someone cut her off on the way home from school. At the end of the story she said that she looked over and saw me in a similar looking car and was relieved to see that it was me. I was so confused! I thought she was saying that I was the one who had cut her off, but she was actually saying that someone else had cut her off and she was afraid to look over at a similar-looking car, which turned out to be me! I was so glad to know I had not cut her off, as I was sure I hadn't cut anyone off, but was genuinely concerned I had! The next time we saw each other in person, we were able to laugh all about this silly mistake. However, even though it was an insignificant misunderstanding, it is a clear example of how difficult it is to clearly communicate online. We couldn't see each other's facial expressions, or quickly clarify if there was a misunderstanding since we typed at different speeds. Then it was tricky because we didn't want to "talk" (type) over each other, and sometimes one person is referring to one topic while the other is thinking about a different idea.

And then there's the whole strategy about responding: when to reply, what to say, and how to word it. In face-to-face interactions, it would be strange to not respond after someone said something to you, or if you asked your friends what to say before responding. On Snapchat, texting, and Instagram, however, there is a whole method of deciding how soon after you receive a notification to respond. Just ask any teenager who uses social media (and even most that don't).

Here's the breakdown of our generation's unspoken etiquette of responding: if the message is one of your closest friends, you respond right away. If the person who contacted you is more of a classmate or acquaintance, they are not your top priority and it is acceptable to reply later (as long as it is on the same day). If someone is reaching out and you are not fond of them at all, usually you wait and respond the next day.

If it is someone with whom you are romantically interested, there is a completely different etiquette. From my experience, usually what goes down is the person receiving the message immediately contacts their closest friends asking for advice (either in person or on over individual text conversations). Eventually, the whole friend group decides together what to say as a reply. This response goes through many changes and drafts before finally coming to a conclusion.

While all of this is going on, the other party can usually see if the message has been read and if the other person is responding-- if the reply takes too long, that is telling of his/her indecisiveness. Sometimes, when the person does not respond, but they have seen the message, it is telling of either their indecision, disinterest, forgetfulness, cautiousness, or value they are placing on the situation. For those who are unfamiliar with this territory, this occurrence is what is known as "being left on read." (On the other hand, if the reply is immediate, then the responder's interest is obvious.)

Once the text is all ready to go, the responder tends to freak out and hesitate, at which point they receive encouragement from their squad (group of close friends helping them through this process). After much consideration and deliberation, the responder (or their friend on their behalf) presses the send button (again, for those unfamiliar, this is known as fully sending it, or a full send). Everyone's heart skips a beat (even if they are not together in person, the friends are most definitely being kept updated through other texts/Snapchats/DMs) and the whole squad waits anxiously for the other person to respond. Then the cycle repeats.

Of course, this system is clearly not fool proof. There is always a possibility that the person receiving the initial message is at a sports practice, an important meeting, or their phone was temporarily taken away. There is no way to be sure, which only adds to the confusion and the likelihood of miscommunication. Suffice it to say, intentions cannot always be clearly interpreted online, thus, increasing the difficulty of being able to effectively communicate.

10: POLITICS

"For social uses, I enjoy it, it keeps people connected. For spreading news about various events, also good. But...for political and other factual means, there is room for improvement. Too many sources have false facts and people can easily spread lies and scams. Social media is a powerful tool that needs to be respected."
-Mike, age 18

#Unsubscribed

10

Since the beginning of time, politics has affected our daily lives. Whether it was the power struggles of trying to become the most powerful country in World War One or the current political climate, politics continue to remain an integral aspect of both our society and our personal lives. Politics obviously influence our countries, laws, taxes, and the overall condition of the world--thus, also affecting our lives individually. In this era of social media, the way politics operate has evolved in ways we have never seen before. Yet because we see the effects day in and day out, we often become accustomed to the integration of politics in social media.

Social media can be informative in the sense that it can spread news rapidly. Yet at the same time, these networks can cause deeper division in our already divided world. In addition to the increased propaganda and ads infiltrating these networking sites, we allow "cookies" on various sites to track us. As we browse, these cookies observe where we obtain our information and which side of the political spectrum we agree with. The sites then show us more and more of our same perspective, which can blind us from looking at both sides. Because of these ads, we may be further polarized from the opposing side and even come to believe our society is more divided than it actually is. We are constantly being exposed to propaganda, yet since it is everywhere online, we are becoming accustomed to it. Since crude political advertisements and political cartoons are relatively normal, we cease to be fully aware of how the propaganda is altering our opinions.

What about fake news? We have all heard the saying, "You can't believe everything you see on the internet." Yet how many of us are quick to believe the adds that pop up on Instagram, Facebook, or in the magazine/explore section of Snapchat, especially if the information lines up with our personal political compass? Here's the kicker: I'm pretty certain that both parties want to help others and do what is best for the situation at hand--we just can't seem to agree on the best way to go about it. Instead of trying to build up from the foundation that we both want what is best, we try to tear each other down. Politics then becomes a competition to see who is right, motives are altered, and we are caught in the middle of a dirty game. That's why, even though we have been told on countless occasions that "you can't believe everything you see on the internet," we still use incorrect information in our arguments. Why? Out of desperation, to prove that one party is better than the other. Does this sound familiar? With this system on social media, usually nobody wins, and everybody loses.

Looking at other people's political views on their social networking accounts can also be detrimental to relationships. Here's how it works: people post about their political perspectives (which you may not agree with). Then you mentally either approve or feel overwhelmed with disgust. You thought you knew them so well, yet how could they be siding with the other party? Traitors.

Knowing which of your friends affiliates with which party can not only alter the dynamic of your relationships (as you may begin to subconsciously think about them differently), but also prevent healthy discussions about politics in the future. Since you found out this information about your friends online, you missed out on an opportunity to learn about how they feel. (Maybe the post misrepresented their beliefs, but it's too late. Now we already have a mental judgment about their philosophies.) Even if you don't agree, if you had this conversation in person, at least you would have a better understanding of why they hold those beliefs. Not only that, but this situation also reduces the chance that you will have future civil conversations about current events, as you would already be defensive going into the conversation knowing that you would have to defend your view. You would be tempted to try to prove the other person wrong and yourself right, because it is no longer about learning about current events and looking to build a compromised solution--it is about becoming the winner.

#Unsubscribed

11: PRIVACY

"I think the topic of social media becomes an even bigger discussion when considering its interaction with politics, news, and privacy issues...When I have kids someday, I will be very cautious and thoughtful about their privacy online and will likely look to another way of sharing family photos with family/friends."
-Catherine, age 27

#Unsubscribed

11

Privacy is something we all yearn for. We may love our friends dearly, but all of our friends don't necessarily know everything about us. For example, one friend may know that I did ballet when I was three-years-old, while another may not; but that second friend might know that I can solve the Rubik's cube, while this is unknown to the first friend. We don't reveal everything about ourselves to any one friend, especially if we do not know them very well. Yet on social media, that's what happens. There are no more secrets; once you post something online, it's out there.

Why, then, do we willingly reveal so much about ourselves in such an accessible way? Even if you have a private account on Instagram, Snapchat, or Facebook, how well do you know the people you let follow you? For most people, they allow their friends to follow them, but also people who may be friends with their friends whom they have never met personally. Woah. So what if one of your friends has a public account? Then anyone can follow them. And if they are asking to follow you, how do you know your friend has actually interacted with them before? It's a trick question: you don't. The problem is, people often get caught up in trying to have more followers. Some people even try to buy followers, to make it seem like they have more friends than they actually do. Why bother? It all ties back to the comparison game.

What do most teenagers have in their Instagram bio? Usually it consists of some form of the school they go to with their graduation year. Even if you are a private account, everyone can still see your bio, regardless of whether or not they follow you. Which means that strangers know your age, and potentially what you look like (depending on what you upload as your profile picture). Yikes!

If you were walking down the street and a stranger asked you how old you are and what school you went to, would you honestly tell them? No! 1) It's creepy. 2) They don't need to know. 3) They could find you. 4) You don't know who they are. 5) You don't know why they want this information. 6) They could be trying to human traffic you. 7) They could find out much more about you with these two simple facts. 8) They could find and hurt your friends or family. There are so many more reasons why you shouldn't tell this stranger about your personal life. So why would you make this information accessible to millions of strangers online? Probably because you want other people from nearby high schools to know they can follow you. But are the extra followers worth the risk? Are they even other high schoolers, or are they fake accounts with people who are just trying to gain your information?

If it is a fake account (which would be really easy to make) with someone who is only following you to try to hurt you or human traffic you, how would you know? More likely than not, you wouldn't. Especially if they are already following one of your other friends. Then let's say you accept them, assuming they are just another high school student from a nearby school. Now they have pictures of you, have pictures of your friends and family, know if you're on vacation (or have the money to go on vacation), know where you have taken your pictures or where you live (if you have the location filter on), and they know who follows you. This could be dangerous not only for you, but it could potentially bring harm to your loved ones. You just never know.

Or perhaps you are following an account that you don't know personally (which most people do, even if it's merely a photography, animal, meme, pun, celebrity/book/movie fan fiction, or inspirational quotes). If you like something, comment on a picture, or even use hashtags* in your own posts (even though they can be fun! #instagram #vscocam #likeforlike #instadaily #photography #blessed

#photooftheday) then hackers can see your interests and can find you from there.

Of course, there is also the issue of colleges. You may have heard those stories of people who are accepted into prestigious universities, but the university decides to withdraw their acceptance because of a photo they found of the person at a party from years ago. Even if you don't post the picture yourself, if you are making poor decisions, it is very likely that a friend documented it with pictures and videos. That friend may post those online, and even if they are deleted later, nothing is ever truly deleted. That one night may cost you your future, because of social media.

What do our social media accounts say about us? How easy would it be for a hacker to find us? What kind of information is there about us online? Who do we let follow us and who do we follow? These are all types of questions that are extremely important to ask, yet are easily forgotten. Social media has the potential to do serious harm--we need to remember to protect our privacy.

#Unsubscribed

*For those of you who are confused as to why I placed
a pound/ number sign in front of those random words,
this is for you. A hashtag (#) is used in social media
(particularly Instagram and Facebook) as an
identifier. For example, if I post a picture of my
family on vacation and in the comments I include
#family, my post will show up with all of the other
posts in which people have also put #family in the
comments. Thus, if you were to be on Instagram and
look up #family, even if you don't follow me, you
could find my post.*

PART THREE
Unstoppable

For the final section of this book, I have provided some of my tips, tricks, and life hacks for unsubscribing. If you are feeling like it might be a good idea to spend less time on social media, this section is for you!

#Unsubscribed

12: NOW WHAT?

"I like it as a way to connect with people and share your life story (in a way), and it's cool to see how other people are doing. However, I do think that it has taken a toll on many people's lives and we need to cut down on the usage of it."
-Madeline, age 15

#Unsubscribed

12

I've shared some thoughts on the inner workings of social media, as well as my personal journey. Now it's your turn. Maybe there was a particular aspect of this book that hit you. Maybe you thought yikes, I feel the exact same way. Maybe you are realizing the amount of time you spend on social media could be used in a different way. Maybe you are sick of it. Maybe you completely disagree with just about everything in this book, but there was that one point that stuck with you. Maybe you have a greater awareness about what goes on inside the world of social media. However you may feel, I urge you to think about it. Force yourself to spend some time thinking in silence, really considering how social media has impacted your life.

If you feel like you have a system figured out and you don't feel consumed or overwhelmed by using social media, that is awesome! That is the goal. I'm not at all here to tell you to stop using social media completely. On the contrary! My hope is that you will be able to find a balance that works for you: **to be able to use social media in moderation.**

If you want to begin reducing your social media usage, here are two tips to get you started: 1) Going cold turkey is hard. If you're feeling extremely motivated, you can try it! But please don't be discouraged if you revert back to your old habits (trust me, I did too). 2) With number one in mind, try to unsubscribe using baby steps, and replace social media with something else! It's hard to remove something completely without having something else to fill the empty space.

In the coming pages, I have included a chart to help get you started. In the boxes with the *"When?"* headers, there are some ideas of times that are perfect opportunities to practice staying off of your phone and living in the moment. In the boxes with the "*How?*" headers, there are some ideas of things you can do to help change your habit of picking up your phone (including fun activities that you can do in the time you might otherwise have used social media!). In other words, this table provides you with a starter pack for how to begin unsubscribing.

Some of these suggestions will definitely work better than others. Find the ones that work for you and stick with them! (As you go along your journey, you will definitely acquire new favorite activities and tricks, too.) Goal setting can also be incredibly helpful. If you decide your perfect balance consists of using social media for 20 minutes every day, give yourself a plan to follow. Where are you going to do it? When are you going to do it? How are you going to hold yourself accountable? Having a plan going into it (and taking baby steps to work up to it) will make your goal much easier to accomplish. If you have a group of friends who want to achieve a similar goal, do it together! That way you can keep each other accountable.

Although setting parameters for how you want to use social media may not always be easy, you can do this! Not only will you be able to live more fully, you will also be exercising your self-control muscle (which is definitely a life skill!). Even if making this change doesn't come easy to you, that is completely normal; don't be discouraged! The important thing is that you're trying-- that's half the battle. If you put in the effort, you will reap the rewards. Who knows, maybe unsubscribing (or being aware of your usage, whatever balance works best for you) will change your life, too.

Unsubscribing Starter Pack

Want to start moderating your social media usage but not sure where to start? The Unsubscribed Starter Pack offers practical tips of how to take the next step in unsubscribing from social media and finding a balance that works for you. You got this!

#Unsubscribed

When?

In the "When?" columns, there are suggestions of times and opportunities to practice staying off your phone and living in the moment.

#Unsubscribed

When?

- Waiting in line

- Waiting to meet up with someone in public

- On the toilet (gross, but true!)

- In the shower

- In the car (of course!), bus, or train

- Brushing your teeth

- Hanging out with friends

- Spending time with family

- While cooking or preparing food

- Eating meals and snacks

- Working on homework, assignments, or other projects that require productivity

- Sports practice/ extracurricular activities

- At the gym or working out

- Outside, in public

- Doing chores (Laundry, dishes, grocery shopping, yard work, etc.)

- During passing period at school

- During break at work

How?

In the "How?" columns, there are ideas of activities and easy ways to fill the time that would otherwise have been spent checking your feed.

#Unsubscribed

How?

- Notice the nature, buildings, and people around you

- Ask someone how their day is going

- Place your phone in another room while you do something else (it eliminates the temptation to use it for procrastination and increases your productivity!)

- Keep a time log of how long you spend on social media each day (or check your settings app)

- Ask yourself why you're logging on before you check your feed

- Sit in a quiet place in silence (or with instrumental music) and practice thinking (try focusing on your breath when your mind wanders!

- Play board games and card games (including solitaire!)

- Go shopping

- Go to the pool, beach, lake, or park; spend time in nature!

- Go hiking

- Try out a new restaurant

- Take a nap (we could all use a little extra sleep!)

- Learn how to do a magic trick

- Learn a new way to do your hair and makeup

- Paint your nails

- Practice playing (or learn to play) an instrument

- Read something (books, poetry, articles, magazines, the newspaper)

- Pray

- Do some journaling

- Write a letter or a hand-written note to someone

- Be creative! Make some artwork!

- Try creative writing

- Cook or bake something

- Exercise

- Learn a new language

- Write down what you're thankful for

- Write a thank you note

- Play with and/or train your pet

- Do a science experiment

- Clean and organize something (maybe a drawer or a shelf in your room)

- Volunteer

- Sew, knit, or quilt!

- Color a coloring page

- Do some karaoke

- *Talk!* Get to know someone (or get closer with your friends) by having some authentic conversations

- Write a book ;)

EPILOGUE:
A BOX OF CHOCOLATES

*"I feel okay about social media! I used to use it
to compare myself with others, but now I'm
comfortable with myself and my life.
So I love it."*
-Ellery, age 16

#Unsubscribed

Epilogue

Social media is like a box of chocolates. Depending on which chocolates we fill the box with, we may find ourselves feeling satisfied or disappointed. We may also spend so much time choosing which chocolates to eat and buy for our boxes, that we have a significant decrease in productivity, and find that we are procrastinating. We may regret the chocolates we picked and compare our choices with our friends'. We may thoroughly enjoy the chocolates while eating them, but then feel awful after eating too many. We may know we shouldn't eat them before mealtime, but do it anyway. We may spend all of our time thinking about whether or not we picked the right ones, and what the number of chocolates we bought says about us. We may feel like the chocolates are consuming us.

Yet we may have begun to realize that these chocolates have the potential to make us feel delighted, too. We may begin to ration them to only a certain number every day. We may even look forward to having our daily treat! We may use it as a connecting point with friends. We may find just the right balance.

> Let's be conscious of how our box of chocolates makes us feel.
> Let's enjoy our chocolates.
> Let's eat our chocolates in moderation.

ACKNOWLEDGEMENTS

#Unsubscribed

ACKNOWLEDGEMENTS

Wow, there are so many incredible people who have helped me along this journey. First and foremost, all glory be to our Lord, Jesus Christ. I am so blessed to be one of His vessels.

To my mom: thank you for doing all of the little things to make sure I have what I need. From making my meals, working hard for our family, and sacrificing your needs for mine, you have always gone above and beyond for me. Thank you for inspiring me to write this book, helping to edit it, and walking with me through this process. I love you.

To my dad: thank you for working so hard for our family. You get up early, you go to bed late, you hardly ever sleep, and usually you work out more than once each day. You are basically superman. Thank you for always supporting me and encouraging me with all my endeavors. With the library of knowledge and experiences in your brain, I have a lot to learn from you. I love you.

To Jake: Thank you for always being my favorite brother. Your actions speak volumes about who you are and your striving for greatness has always inspired me to become a better and more confident version of myself. You are a beast (both mentally and physically) and I'm honored to be your sister. I love you.

Thank you to my extended family--I undoubtedly have the best family in the world. I appreciate your support and love as I journey through life; I love you all so much.

Thank you to my friends, past and present; each one of you have taught me about life through the memories we have made together. You hold a special place in my heart and nothing can ever replace our adventures.

Thank you to all of the teachers and mentors I've had throughout the years. You have helped me grow, challenged me, and shaped the way I see the world. You are incredibly important--not just to me, but to all of the people you interact with. You have the potential to influence people's lives; please use your opportunity to change our world for the better.

Thank you to all of those whose hard work and dedication make our world better, yet often go unnoticed. I appreciate your sacrifices.

Thank you to every single person who read this book. I am so grateful to you for taking the time to look at the world through my eyes. I hope you were able to find take-aways that are applicable to your life.

Thank you to all of you who have helped shape me into who I am today.

I am truly blessed.

#Unsubscribed

ABOUT THE AUTHOR

#Unsubscribed

ABOUT THE AUTHOR

Alexa Mendes is a 16-year-old student entering her junior year of high school. She was named Student-of-the-Year at both her elementary and middle schools, and continues to strive for excellence today. She has a 4.0 GPA and is greatly involved in her community. At her church, Alexa helps with religious education, has been a leader for the youth group, and is a proclaimer of the word. At school, Alexa loves to be a part of the ASB class and was even elected as Sophomore Director, thus planning her school's winter formal for around 1,000 people.

Having played basketball throughout her youth, she has also won various championships and ultimately made her school's Varsity basketball team both freshman and sophomore years. As a freshman, her team won the regional championship for the first time in her school's history and then once again made it to the regional finals in her sophomore year.

Additionally, Alexa has been a Girl Scout for more than 11 years, earning her Bronze, Silver, and Gold Awards. For her Gold Award, the highest award a Girl Scout can earn (equivalent to a Boy Scout becoming an Eagle Scout), Alexa tackled the issue of stress. Identifying the root cause of stress as the lack of awareness of healthy ways to manage stress, Alexa compiled 8 quick-and-easy stress relieving techniques and led her team to transform them into booklets (in French, English, and Spanish) and accompanying videos. She then led a team to present these techniques and the availability of these resources to the 1800 students at her school. Knowing stress is a global issue, Alexa and her team members shared these techniques with people across the world. All of these resources continue to remain accessible for free on her website, www.breathetorelieve.weebly.com.

Questions?
Comments?
Feedback?

Connect with Alexa!

unsubscribedbook@gmail.com
www.unsubscribedbook.weebly.com
www.breathetorelieve.weebly.com

53190803R00093

Made in the USA
San Bernardino, CA
12 September 2019